Cole, Joanna.
The Clown-Arounds have a party

DATE DUE

APR 1 9 1995	JUL 1 0 1996	SEP 2 7 2002
MAY 0 5 1995	JUL 2 6 1996	MAR 3 1 2003
MAY 2 2 1995	JUL 3 1 1996	
MAY 2 6 1995	MAY 1 9 1997	
JUN 0 7 1995	MAR 0 4 1998	
JUN 1 9 1995	APR 1 7 1998	
OCT 0 3 1995	JUN 1 9 1998	
OCT 1 3 1995	JUL 0 1 1998	
OCT 2 7 1995	JAN 0 4 1999	
APR 1 0 1996	APR 1 9 2000	
APR 2 2 1996	OCT 0 8 2001	
JUN 0 5 1996	AUG 1 9 2002	

THE CLOWN-AROUNDS HAVE A PARTY

To librarians, parents, and teachers:

The Clown-Arounds Have a Party is a Parents Magazine READ ALOUD Original — one title in a series of colorfully illustrated and fun-to-read stories that young readers will be sure to come back to time and time again.

Now, in this special school and library edition of *The Clown-Arounds Have a Party*, adults have an even greater opportunity to increase children's responsiveness to reading and learning — and to have fun every step of the way.

When you finish this story, check the special section at the back of the book. There you will find games, projects, things to talk about, and other educational activities designed to make reading enjoyable by giving children and adults a chance to play together, work together, and talk over the story they have just read.

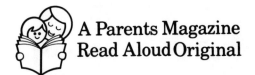

The Clown-Arounds Have a Party

For a free color catalog describing Gareth Stevens' list of high-quality books, call 1-800-542-2595 (USA) or 1-800-461-9120 (Canada). Gareth Stevens' Fax: (414) 225-0377.

Parents Magazine READ ALOUD Originals:

A Garden for Miss Mouse
Aren't You Forgetting
  Something, Fiona?
Bicycle Bear
Bicycle Bear Rides Again
The Biggest Shadow in
  the Zoo
Bread and Honey
Buggly Bear's Hiccup Cure
But No Elephants
Cats! Cats! Cats!
The Cat's Pajamas
Clara Joins the Circus
The Clown-Arounds
The Clown-Arounds Go
  on Vacation
The Clown-Arounds Have
  a Party
Elephant Goes to School
The Fox with Cold Feet
Get Well, Clown-Arounds!
The Ghost in Dobbs Diner
The Giggle Book
The Goat Parade

Golly Gump Swallowed a Fly
Henry Babysits
Henry Goes West
Henry's Awful Mistake
Henry's Important Date
The Housekeeper's Dog
I'd Like to Be
The Little Witch Sisters
The Man Who Cooked
  for Himself
Milk and Cookies
Miss Mopp's Lucky Day
No Carrots for Harry!
Oh, So Silly!
The Old Man and the
  Afternoon Cat
One Little Monkey
The Peace-and-Quiet Diner
The Perfect Ride
Pets I Wouldn't Pick
Pickle Things
Pigs in the House
Rabbit's New Rug
Rupert, Polly, and Daisy

Sand Cake
Septimus Bean and His
  Amazing Machine
Sheldon's Lunch
Sherlock Chick and the
  Giant Egg Mystery
Sherlock Chick's First Case
The Silly Tail Book
Snow Lion
Socks for Supper
Sweet Dreams,
  Clown-Arounds!
Ten Furry Monsters
There's No Place Like Home
This Farm is a Mess
Those Terrible Toy-Breakers
Up Goes Mr. Downs
The Very Bumpy Bus Ride
Where's Rufus?
Who Put the Pepper in
  the Pot?
Witches Four

Library of Congress Cataloging-in-Publication Data

Cole, Joanna.
     The Clown-Arounds have a party / by Joanna Cole ; pictures by
Jerry Smath.
         p. cm. -- (Parents magazine read aloud original)
     Summary: The funniest family in town pulls some of its best high
jinks to cheer up homesick Cousin Fizzy.
     ISBN 0-8368-0999-8
     [1. Clowns--Fiction. 2. Homesickness--Fiction.] I. Smath,
Jerry, ill. II. Title. III. Series.
PZ7.C67346Cm 1995
[E]--dc20   94-34652

This North American library edition published in 1995 by Gareth Stevens Publishing, 1555 North RiverCenter Drive, Suite 201, Milwaukee, Wisconsin, 53212, USA, under an arrangement with Gruner + Jahr USA Publishing.

Printed in the United States of America

1 2 3 4 5 6 7 8 9 99 98 97 96 95

The Clown-Arounds Have a Party

by Joanna Cole   pictures by Jerry Smath

Parents Magazine Press
New York

Gareth Stevens Publishing
MILWAUKEE

To my brothers, Joe, John,
and Jim (Krenshaw) Smath—J.S.

Do you know the Clown-Arounds?
They're the funniest family in town.

There's Mrs. Clown-Around,
Mr. Clown-Around,
their daughter, Bubbles,
the Baby,
and Wag-Around, their dog.

11

Everything about the Clown-Arounds
is funny.

Their dinner plates,

their lamp,

their rug,

even their refrigerator!

But nothing is as funny as
the Clown-Arounds themselves.
They are always playing tricks
on each other.

They like to tell jokes and riddles.

And they love to act silly.
Uh-oh. It's silly time again
at the Clown-Arounds' house.

19

One weekend, Cousin Fizzy came
to visit the Clown-Arounds.
They gave him a big hello.
Bubbles gave him a hand
with his suitcase, too.

The Clown-Arounds invited Fizzy
to come in and sit down.
Everyone was having a good time . . .

23

But then Fizzy started feeling homesick.

So Bubbles tried extra hard
to show Fizzy a good time.

27

Baby offered Fizzy a special treat.

Even Wag-Around
tried to help.

But nothing worked.
Fizzy still felt homesick,
so he went to take a nap.

Then Bubbles
got an idea.

While Fizzy was asleep,
the Clown-Arounds hopped into their car.
They almost got lost . . .

But finally they found the right place.
They got a big welcome.

Then they packed up their car
and started home.

WHAT KIND OF JAM
DOESN'T GO ON BREAD?

A TRAFFIC JAM!

37

They got back in the nick of time.
Fizzy was just waking up.

Now he had no reason to be homesick.

So Fizzy joined the fun.

The Clown-Arounds think that the
best way to spend a weekend
is to have a house party.
Don't you?

Notes to Grown-ups

Major Themes
Here is a quick guide to the significant themes and concepts at work in *The Clown-Arounds Have a Party*:

- Making a guest feel welcome, as the clown family tried to do.
- Language can be just for fun, as shown here by the nonsense and amusing plays on words.

Step-by-step Ideas for Reading and Talking
Here are some ideas for further give-and-take between grown-ups and children. The following topics encourage creative discussion of *The Clown-Arounds Have a Party* and invite the kind of open-ended response that is consistent with many contemporary approaches to reading, including Whole Language:

- The pictures in Clown-Around books do more than just illustrate the words. They tell some of the story, and they play jokes on the words. Example: the "hand" Bubbles gives his cousin. Closely examine all the pictures with your child, looking for such wordplay.

- Being homesick may be a new idea to your child. Some kids think it means being sick at home, or even sick *of* home! But they may remember being glad to return home after a trip, and this memory might help them understand how Fizzy felt.

44

Games for Learning

Games and activities can stimulate young readers and listeners alike to find out more about words, numbers, and ideas. Here are more ideas for turning learning into fun:

Clown Hat Place Markers

To make clown hat place markers, top the pointed end of pointed ice cream cones with a yarn pom-pom. Print the names of family members or guests on small pieces of of paper and use glue or paste to affix name tags to the base of the cones. Invert the hats and position them around the table as place markers or cards.

Dirt Cake

Find the hat that Bubbles Clown-Around is wearing in this book. Then you and your child can make a Dirt Cake together, decorated to look like Bubbles's hat. Wash a clay flowerpot and line it with aluminum foil. Then fill the pot, following this recipe:

- 1 large package of chocolate sandwich cookies
- 1/2 stick of margarine (softened)
- 8 ounces (230 grams) cream cheese (softened)
- 1 cup (110 g) powdered sugar
- 3 1/2 cups (.84 liters) milk
- 2 packages instant French vanilla pudding
- 12 ounces (345 g) frozen whipped topping

(continued on page 48)

In a bowl, mix the margarine, cream cheese, and powdered sugar. In a separate bowl, mix the milk, pudding mix, and whipped topping. Then fold the two creamy mixtures together. Crush the cookies, and place a layer of cookie crumbs in the bottom of the lined pot, then add a layer of the cream mix. Continue with a layer of cookies, then cream, then cookies. Stick a silk flower into your dirt cake and refrigerate overnight. For added fun, you could put in a gummy worm or two, and then serve your "dirt cake" with a small, clean garden trowel!

About the Author

JOANNA COLE enjoys writing the stories and inventing the jokes that appear in the Clown-Around books. "But Jerry Smath's illustrations are still a surprise," says Ms. Cole. "He always comes up with something I didn't think of. That's the fun and privilege of working with a terrific artist."

Joanna Cole was an elementary schoolteacher and a children's book editor before she turned to writing full time. She has written both fiction and nonfiction books for children, a nonfiction book for grown-ups, and numerous magazine articles. Ms. Cole lives with her husband and daughter in New York City.

About the Artist

JERRY SMATH does free-lance illustration for magazines and children's books. He wrote and illustrated two books for Parents, *But No Elephants* and *The Housekeeper's Dog*. He also illustrated *The Clown-Arounds* by Joanna Cole. "When I work with an author," says Mr. Smath, "we must both think and feel like children for the book to turn out right!"

Mr. Smath and his wife, Valerie, a graphic designer, live in Westchester County, New York.